# Table of Conten

MW01077983

# Oppositional Defiant Disorder

*How to Manage and Treat a Child with ODD*

by Joseph Stenson

# Introduction

"Kyle, go pick up those toys," Mary demands.

"No!" her five-year-old son responds.

"Kyle, you need to pick them up now," Mary says, getting a bit agitated.

"No!" Kyle replies with his arms folded.

Now Mary has just about lost it, and yells at the top of her lungs, "For the last time, Kyle Daryl Sullivan, GO PICK UP YOUR TOYS!"

Kyle screams, "NO!" and then runs away.

Mary stands there, scratching her head. Where did her parenting skills go wrong? She doesn't spoil her children or give in to all their demands. She's raised two children prior to Kyle, and they turned out to be perfectly well-mannered and even tempered. But Kyle is different. He is usually pouty, often disobedient, and habitually displays anger and resentment, not only towards his family, but also towards his classmates, his teacher at school, and other children and adults. What can be done about Kyle?

To a lot of parents who've had to deal with difficult children, Mary's story is all too familiar. You may be struggling to find effective solutions to help you deal with this problem. Seeking advice from friends and relatives, in addition to being uncomfortable, may also prove ineffective, seeing as most parents have truly never encountered the same magnitude of persistent obstinate behavior in their own children.

If you are experiencing this problem, you are not alone. Your "unruly" child or teenager may have a clinically classified condition known as oppositional defiance disorder (ODD). ODD is characterized by persistent behaviors and attitudes of negativity, defiance, and disobedience. ODD children are also seemingly hardwired to push back hard against any authoritative presence, including parents and teachers.

## Aren't Children and Teenagers Defiant By Nature?

While it's completely natural for children (especially teenagers) to challenge authority, the ODD diagnosis is meant to help identify teenagers and children whose impulse to defy has outpaced other critical maturation points. These maturation points include the ability to be patient, the ability to cultivate trust, the ability to compromise etc. The simplest way to differentiate between a normal child's or adolescent's challenges to authority and ODD is by assessing the child's behavior over the course of a significant period of time. Most psychologists think that an appropriate assessment time period is six months in order to warrant the ODD diagnosis. The six month time-frame allows parents and psychologists to distinguish between isolated episodes – such as tantrums resulting from the child not getting what he wants – and chronic dispositions of defiance.

## ODD Symptoms

Consistent temper tantrums, arguing with adults, failing to comply with rules and requests made by adults, annoying people on purpose, being easily agitated and angry, as well as exhibiting vindictiveness are all possible indicators of ODD.

Some of the standard ODD symptoms can also help differentiate between normal, occasional oppositional behavior—the kind found in most children—and what would be classified as ODD. In short, the ODD children exhibit an excessive degree of mean and even hateful behavior. They usually have little or no qualms about using the worst, most obscene, most hurtful language they know in order to get their point across. ODD children are also more inclined to pursue revenge. It's as if they've lost a kind of innocence, and have come to prematurely understand and leverage spite and cruelty long before they've developed mature empathetic abilities to counter these darker impulses. This is not to say that ODD children are sociopathic; they truly believe that their behavior is justified and that everyone else is to blame for not adopting their distinct view of reality.

When a child has ODD, he will often be persistently stubborn, resist any request or directive made by an adult, be unwilling to compromise or negotiate with adults, or even his peers. He will do things for no other apparent reason other than to test your patience and cross boundaries and will refuse to accept any accountability for his actions.

## Ground-Zero of the ODD Diagnosis

ODD symptoms will usually manifest in the home setting, and it's often the parents who seek professional intervention first. On rare occasions, the child's teacher or school administrator will be the one to suggest that the child be screened professionally.

If left unattended, ODD behaviors will cause the child to suffer socially, academically, and emotionally. Even if you've consulted the latest DSM manual, WebMD, and this book, don't attempt to diagnose your child on your own. If your child displays common ODD symptoms, take him to a psychologist or psychiatrist to obtain proper testing and diagnoses.

Fortunately, ODD is treatable, and with proper guidance, you can help your child improve and cope with the underlying factors that create this condition. There are also specialized training curriculums available for parents with ODD children. This training can be costly, but it can also be conducted in a group setting, which helps to lower costs while fostering social support. During these training sessions, you will learn different techniques that can be used to maintain clear-headed constructive control in various situations as they arise with your child. Family therapy is also, in some cases, an effective solution. In terms of medication, there are none tailored to this disorder. Research in this field is still new and ongoing.

This book will help parents of ODD children who are looking for practical, here-and-now solutions to support their children while maintaining a peaceful and cooperative home environment.

# Chapter 1: Beginning With What You Can Control

*A soft answer turns away wrath, but grievous words stir up anger.*

- Hebrew Proverb

*God, grant me the serenity to accept the things I cannot change,*

*The courage to change the things I can,*

*And the wisdom to know the difference.*

- Originally coined by the Theologian, Reinhold Niebuhr, later adapted by Alcoholics Anonymous

Let's not kid ourselves. All parents get angry with their children. You get frustrated. You lose your patience. You say things you regret saying. You're not proud of it. You don't like to admit it, but when you've got stressors coming from work, spouses, or other children, and then you add an ODD child into the mix, things can spin out of control easily.

The great irony here is that when your child is suffering from ODD, it's even more important that you stay in firm control of your own emotions. If you, as a parent, resort to spitefulness, extreme negativity, or worse, physical violence, it will only confirm the validity of his behavior as an effective and normal means for getting what he wants. If you're raising an ODD child and have a tendency to lose your patience quickly, then you owe it to yourself to seek counseling. Regularly seeing a counsellor will give you the time and space during which you and your needs will be the center of attention. Having this space could prove critical for a parent who's exerting an extreme amount of patience on the home front. Even if you're not having trouble controlling the expression of your emotions at home, raising an ODD child comes with a large amount of emotional wear and tear on the parent. It's perfectly acceptable, and encouraged, to seek professional support for yourself.

One of the mistakes parents make is waiting until an extremely significant, dangerous, or catastrophic event takes place before they seek professional help for themselves. If you believe your child may be ODD, then don't wait for an official diagnosis or for something bad to happen, get support as soon as you can. Dealing with a child with ODD can be very stressful, and failing to find support results in putting you, your child, and the rest of your family members at risk. Caring for a child with ODD is going to be one of the most difficult challenges you'll ever take on. You have to be on top form, and a good therapist will help you get there.

There are numerous therapists' practices, programs and classes that cater for people looking to manage stress and anger. Therapy sessions, though often effective, can also be expensive. A cheaper alternative is anger management classes, where a group of people share individual experiences and offer tips and ways in which each member of the group successfully addresses anger-related issues. As long as you're actively building solutions for better self-control and also accessing a human support network, you're going to be in a much better position, emotionally, to take on the challenge of an ODD child.

## Stay Calm and In Control

It is only in your calmest moments that you're capable of handling your child intelligently. Unbridled emotions have a way of overriding cognitive portions of your brain when you're attempting to make decisions and you end up making poor choices.

Parents who are able to control their emotions when dealing with an ODD child are able to subtly establish leadership in the relationship. You may not be able to control what your child says or does, but you can show him how problems can be resolved in a calm and civil manner. Failing to keep composure and giving in to anger can result in you losing both your self-respect and all credibility with your child.

Let's consider the plight of a Rhonda, from Thousand Oaks California. Rhonda's story— though based on an actual situation involving a Southern California woman raising an ODD child—has been altered slightly to protect her identity. Rhonda's teenager, Jacob, had such extraordinary anger that he would regularly sneak up behind his mother and grab her by the neck and pretend, quite convincingly, to choke her when he was in a foul mood. This was a bizarre, dangerous behavior and one of many ODD symptoms that Jacob exhibited. Having been expelled from his high school for physically assaulting a teacher, Jacob spent countless hours with his xBox, playing violent shoot-em-up video games. He refused to do any work around the house and maintained a consistent attitude of disrespect and anger towards both his father and mother. Jacob's father, Clint, had always been the more passive and dismissive parent when it came to Jacob's behavior. Clint's softer, deferential approach to handling Jacob seemed to feed Jacob's anger. Meanwhile, Rhonda, feeling unsupported by her husband in the midst of an incredibly trying situation, was on the brink of filing for divorce. Rhonda had come from an abusive home, with an alcoholic father who couldn't contain his own anger. Seeing shades of her own father in Jacob, who, at 17, was also prone to abusing alcohol and drugs, left Rhonda in a state of despair. And then, one day, *she* lost control.

It happened during one of Jacob's tirades, apparently the result of becoming frustrated by a video game. Jacob stormed into the living room and kicked Junior, the family's golden retriever. The dog yelped. Rhonda, aghast, screamed at him, "Jacob!"

"Fuck off," was his prompt and snide response.

Before she knew what she was doing, Rhonda slammed her son up against the wall and struck him repeatedly with flailing arms, elbows, and fists. Jacob was so stunned by the behavior that he didn't even attempt a violent response—quite uncharacteristic for him—but wriggled away from his mother's assault and screamed at her, "You crazy bitch!" before retreating back into his room behind a slammed door.

Some parents' violent reactions arise from deeper issues, rooted in their own childhood. We all enter parenthood with wounds, and some of us, like Rhonda, have been more deeply traumatized than others. The ODD child has a way of unknowingly opening up your old wounds, which in turn spurs forth impulses to negative reactions. Sometimes your knee-jerk responses are so deeply ingrained in your psyche that you barely have a chance at controlling yourself. Such negative reactions can harm the child, and eventually may even shape his future with his own children. This cycle of emotional baggage, and abuse, can continue indefinitely across multiple generations.

Sounds like quite a dire outlook, but let's see if there is a bright-side to all of this. As a parent of an ODD child, you're inevitably going to be put in a situation where your own baggage is brought to the surface. But now you're dealing with your issues as an adult and have more control over what happens to you and more awareness with regard to how to process these feelings that you've not felt since your own childhood. If you think about it, this is an incredible opportunity for you.

*A pessimist sees the difficulty in every opportunity; an optimist sees the opportunity in every difficulty.*

- Winston Churchill

The challenge you're facing in dealing with an ODD child, when optimistically contextualized, is a chance to break a deeply, perhaps genetically, ingrained destructive cycle. Every step you take towards breaking this cycle, including reading this book, should be considered a heroic act.

So now that we have established the dangers of resorting to anger-motivated responses to your child, here are some ways in which you can keep your anger in check:

## 1. Know When Too Far is Too Far

Understanding your limits is one of the best ways to keep your anger in check. When we angrily go after our children, it is usually because we haven't set limits for ourselves when it comes to how we intend to deal with our children. It's important that these personal, self-controlled limits are established and abided by consistently. Some parents, for example, determine that they will never discipline their children by spanking but by confiscating coveted possessions, or rewarding good behavior. Other parents decide that spanking is okay, as long as it's not undertaken while the parent is angry.

There's no perfect parenting philosophy, and different approaches work with different children. But most parents and psychologists agree that consistency and boundaries are important. To help you reflect on and clearly define appropriate limits for discipline, sit down and create a list—use a note-taking app on your phone, or even use a Post-It sticker—of disciplinary measures that are acceptable, and those that are never permissible. Read over your limits on a regular basis. Remember, these limits may not be intuitive to you, especially in the heat of anger, as you may not have been raised in a household where such limits were applied.

If you're instinctually inclined to express anger, don't feel bad about it. It's perfectly normal. You just need to find an alternative channel to vent through. Make another list and write down ways that you can deal with anger and the other negative emotions that are inevitably going to arise as you struggle to deal with your ODD child. Some ideas may include: going for a walk, playing some calming music, meditating, or just locking yourself in your room for a while and taking some personal time. It's also, as previously mentioned, helpful to have a counsellor to talk to.

## 2. Recognize and Prevent False Alarms

When you're dealing with a child that constantly presses your buttons, you may, at times, find yourself inclined to blame things on him or her, even when it's not warranted. Many times, as a parent, you'll see your child doing something questionable, or out of the ordinary, and you'll instantly become upset or angry about it. "Cut it out," you'll say to a child who's adding enthused audio commentary to the drama unfolding in his Lego set. He's just a child playing with Legos, but in your mind, for a split second, he's being unruly, and you want him to knock it off.

At times like these it's helpful to take an introspective moment. Perhaps you're irritable because you've had a rough day at work, or maybe you've got a headache, and your child is annoying you just by being, well, childish. Misplaced anger is a phenomenon present not only in a parent-child relationships, but in several other social settings. It's especially critical to be aware of your behavior and potential misplaced anger when dealing with an ODD child, because you've likely become so habituated to scolding your child that it's become second nature.

Not only will you feel badly if you go off on your child when he doesn't deserve it, but you will also adversely affect any efforts your child is making to improve his behavior. When you're inclined to scold your child after a rough day at work or after a trying event, stop and reflect for a minute on what's really irritating you. If the child's behavior truly requires discipline or correction, then simply approach your child as you would normally, in a calm and controlled manner. Remind him of the rules that have been established. Phrase your instruction by letting him know what you need from him — I need you to etc. This phrasing puts him in a position of feeling important, and will make him feel valued.

Don't be cynical and think that just because your child is ODD that he doesn't care at all about pleasing you. He cares, he just often believes that it's not possible, so he succumbs to despair, anger and helplessness. Tell him exactly what he can do to please you and address him with a firm calmness. You may be surprised at his responsiveness.

## 3. Isolate Yourself

This may be the most effective means of letting go of your anger. When you are separated from the source of the problem, then you will be able to let go of your anger more quickly. Isolate yourself by locking yourself in the bathroom or the bedroom, and count to ten, listen to music, read a book, or pray. Do whatever you need to do to keep your emotions under control. When you have calmed down, you can return to dealing with your child.

## 4. Avoid Reacting Physically

If your aim is to maintain a clear, calm, and controlled response when dealing with your ODD child, then you should strive to avoid spanking. Spanking can easily escalate to more damaging whippings and beatings, especially when dealing with an ODD child. If you must spank, always do so at least 15 minutes after the incident has taken place. Make sure that you're not spanking while fueled by anger and adrenaline.

Though spanking is used as a disciplinary tool in over 80% of American homes (according to the American Academy of Pediatrics), it's come into strong disfavor among psychological professionals. In Irwin A. Hyman's groundbreaking, *The Case Against Spanking*, Hyman notes how one of the most appalling practices of white settlers, as observed by native Americans in the 15th and 16th centuries, was hitting of children by parents. Though it's deeply ingrained in our culture, it's not necessarily an optimal approach to discipline.

You may resort to physical punishment because it was used to discipline you when you were growing up. When considering the use of corporal punishment, as an adult, in your own household, it's important to reflect on the feelings of low self-worth that you may have experienced in your own childhood. These are the feelings commonly associated with being spanked or whipped as a child.

Many parents are inclined to refer to their having, "turned out fine," when they want to justify spanking, and even whipping (the repetitive striking of a child with a hairbrush, whip, or similar tool). In actuality, no one is fine. You carry some emotional scarring, regardless of whether you were spanked or not, regardless of whether you've enjoyed healthy adult lives or not. Surviving any kind of abuse does not justify the abuse. Learning to discipline without spanking can break a chain of emotional scarring, especially when it comes to dealing with ODD children, who need more than anything, positive examples of how problems can be resolved without resorting to anger and violence.

Unfortunately, physical punishment on an ODD child usually results in more resistance, more defiance of authority, and generally more acting out in inappropriate, aggressive, hostile, and violent ways.

## 5. Consider Better Methods for Disciplining Your Child

So, if you can't yell or spank a child with ODD, then what can you do? Punishing a child, though necessary, is always going to be a form of negative reinforcement. The best ways to punish will equate the negative reinforcement with the lack of a positive reinforcement or reward. One idea you can try is the use of allowances.

Allowances are privileges the child receives that are contingent on cooperative behavior. Once the child ceases to be cooperative, then the allowance is revoked. In Rhonda's case, seeing how her ODD teenager, Jacob, loved to play video games, using his access to the video game console or television would have served as the perfect allowance. When Jacob behaved disrespectfully or refused to do his assigned chores, his video game privileges will be taken away.

When setting up an allowance system for your child, be sure to take the opportunity to sit down and discuss how the system is going to work with him. You want to be perfectly clear about what's expected of the child and what the consequences will be for his failure to fulfill the expectations. Prepare yourself, an ODD child will object to every aspect of your proposal. You have to trust that the system you're laying out is fair and stick to your guns. Don't let your child bait you into an argument or debate.

An ODD child will thoroughly test your resolve to stick to your allowances program. He will feel out any vague or gray area of your set-forth requirements and exploit it relentlessly. If part of his responsibility is to sweep the driveway once a week. Be prepared for him to make a half-hearted and incomplete effort. How are you going to respond? If he's required to study for at least an hour every evening, how are you going to ensure that he does so? If you have a parenting partner, sit down with him or her and think through every dimension and contingency of your plan, then execute it.

## 6. Privately Empathize with Your Child's Predicament

One way in which you can maintain your equanimity and reign in the impulse to anger, is by thoughtfully and regularly putting yourself in your child's shoes. If your ODD child is still very young, imagine how it might seem threatening when someone, three times bigger than him, tells him he's doing something wrong. Because of his disorder he has trouble trusting and deferring to your guidance and instructions and the only response that makes sense to him is emphatic resistance.

Brain scans have shown that the brains of children with ODD have key neurological differences in the areas which control impulsivity and judgment. Even though your child may not be telegraphing that he's afraid and confused and unsure of himself, that's very likely exactly what's going on inside his mind. Your child may see you as a lightning rod, there to absorb all of his angst and resentment towards a world he doesn't understand.

When you show anger while dealing with your ODD child, this leads him to identify an area in his life where his influence and power is truly felt and he will continue to provoke you so as to feel that level of control and importance again. No, you can't control everything as a parent, but you can control some things. You can control the way you respond to a challenging predicament and when dealing with a child with ODD, your best approach is staying in control of yourself. This means remaining calm, communicating clearly, disciplining in a consistent fashion with clear limitations drawn, and finding constructive, safe ways to deal with your own natural anger.

# Chapter 2: Procuring Professional Help for Your Child

Now that you're doing everything you can to help yourself and are effectively dealing with the baggage you're bringing home, it's time to think about finding some professional help for your ODD child. Just like you, your child should have a safe, impartial space to express his own feelings about his life at home, school and in general. A professional counsellor or psychologist can also help your child develop different and constructive solutions to address various problems he may be facing.

Many parents believe in the falsehood that they alone should offer guidance to their children. Hence, they don't believe that taking their children to a psychologist or psychiatrist is a prudent decision. In fact, some parents think that seeking professional intervention for their child is the mark of incompetence or disinterest in doing their own parenting. They believe that since they're the parents, they themselves should be capable of sorting out any behavioral problems using their own parenting skills. Oddly though, parents with this attitude towards professional intervention are more than willing to take their child to a pediatrician if he's got the flu or chicken pox. So why is it that when a child displays distinct signs of a classified and researched mental or emotional disorder—where, just as in medicine, a body of evidence exists that says professional intervention can result in improvement—parents suddenly feel they should oversee the entire course of treatment for their child by themselves? There is still a stigma and distrust associated with counselling and psychological services, and it's unfortunate, because the result is that only one in five children gets treated for mental illnesses like ODD.

## When to Seek Help

Don't wait for a watershed moment, when you-know-what hits the fan. Though major blow-ups, for many parents, are the wake-up call they need, it's not worth allowing your child and the rest of your family to experience a traumatic event before you reach out for help. Compared to having a child in trouble with the law, or having a child injure someone or sustain an injury themselves, the so-called stigma of seeking professional help is miniscule. Seek help before you've exhausted all your options in dealing with your ODD child.

In preparation for finding a suitable counsellor you'll need to put in some research time. Remember, your child's relationship with a counsellor is not just about getting the proper diagnosis but will be an ongoing routine of regular visits with the goal of remedying, or at least abating, your child's disorder. In the meantime, if you're continuing to work out your own issues, you will be steadily becoming a better parent and a better person. The right amount of give from both the child and the parent can produce very powerful and lasting positive results.

## *What stigma?*

There are many reasons parents cite for not taking their children to get treated for psychological disturbances such as ODD. Many parents erroneously think that taking their child in for treatment not only makes them failures as parents, but it also threatens to bestow a stigma upon the child. Some parents mistakenly think that if their child is diagnosed as "ODD" that it equates to a mark of shame. The fundamental misunderstanding here is that diagnoses such as ODD were created to provide an infrastructure for treatment. The poorer parental choice would be not taking advantage of this available infrastructure. Mental health issues remain one of the most stigmatized health problems, and this is why people neglect and postpone seeking professional intervention for themselves and their family members, even when the justification for such a course of action is abundantly clear.

What makes this perceived stigma a great tragedy is that the failure to obtain the proper support could result in the problems worsening, or even culminating in severe injury or self-harm. Do not be afraid to take your child in for help. Licensed guidance counsellors, psychologists, and psychiatrists are trained professionals who are already spending the better part of each day learning about and confronting problems similar to yours, and they could become a valuable partner for you and your child as you confront the difficulties of ODD.

If you're at all concerned about confidentiality and privacy, keep in mind that members of the psychological services profession have sworn an oath to keep any shared information confidential. This oath is serious and can only be broken if the therapist is somehow made privy to information about someone's life being in jeopardy. Failure to uphold privacy standards could spell disaster for the careers of these professionals. You are thus free to discuss your situation with them, with 100% assurance of confidentiality.

Another reason parents give for not taking their child to a therapist is that the child refuses to go. This is not uncommon. Most people, adults included, don't enjoy going to therapy. To deal with your child's reservation, you need to take the lead. Remember, children need you to guide them, even though they'll never admit it and often don't act like it. You should be the voice of clear reason and judgment. In order to effectively get your child to attend treatment, you must encourage the child to go to therapy sessions in a positive and meaningful way. While you shouldn't directly compare going to therapy to going to school, you should persuade your child using the same matter-of-fact manner that you'd use when telling her to go out and catch the school bus. Use the phrase, *"It's just something you need to do."* Parents may also want to provide incentives for their children to attend therapy, such as the promise of going somewhere special afterwards.

Many child therapists will lighten the persuasion burden on parents by making therapy more fun for children. They do this by incorporating activities and games into their sessions. Drawing pictures is a very common technique therapists use not only to make therapy more interesting for children, but also to get to know them better. Child therapists like to talk to children about their artwork and the inspirations behind it. For smaller children, therapists keep more simple toys on-hand. Between the fun environment for children provided by therapists and the positive, insistent persuasion efforts from parents, a weekly visit to a trusted therapist can easily become part of the normal routine.

Be careful with the methods you use to entice your children to go to therapy. Even though children will bristle at the idea of going to see a professional "Doctor" of any kind for fear of shots or other frightening procedures, you shouldn't spring the news on them during the car ride to the therapist's office. Give your child a chance to ask questions and express his opinions. If your child is ODD, then, of course, expect resistance, but use firm but positive encouragement. Another bad habit parents can be tempted to succumb to is framing therapy as a kind of punishment, i.e. telling a child that if she doesn't behave as expected that she'll be taken back to the therapist. Such poorly conceived framing only helps to reinforce one of the most destructive misnomers about therapy—that kids are taken to therapy because they're bad.

## How to Find a Therapist

Another excuse which parents use is that they are unable to find any healthcare professionals within reasonable geographic proximity. If you live in a rural area, then you should search the web or the yellow pages for your nearest psychotherapist. In most areas of the country, you should be able to find a therapist within a reasonable distance, but if you are not looking for them, then you will not see them.

A great way to find a therapist is by way of referral. If you're fortunate enough to have a school teacher, principal, guidance counselor, or pediatrician you trust, then you've a good chance of getting a good recommendation for a therapist within reach. Even family members can give you recommendations. You just have to ask around. There are many professionals who are licensed to support you and your child as you tackle the problem of ODD including psychiatrists, psychologists, social workers, marriage and family counselors, and even some spiritual leaders.

## Dealing with Therapy Costs

Expense is another excuse that parents make too often when refusing to even look for professional help. The truth of the matter is as simple as seek and you will find. While the cost of therapy can be a significant problem for some families, solutions are available and you need to seek them out. There are many lower-cost clinics that offer the same services as private services but at half the price. Also, if you have health insurance— which, thanks to Health Care Reform should be within financial reach for every American—then you may be legally entitled to receive coverage for counselling and psychotherapy. Talk to your insurance provider and find out the facts. You can also take your child to group therapy sessions. While group therapy won't provide your child with the same level of focused, individual attention, it's administered by a licensed professional and can be very helpful, especially if your child is having trouble socializing with others his age. Since group therapy divides the time of the professional therapist over multiple clients, the overall cost is lower.

Keep looking and asking questions. When you approach a therapist whose services you're interested in, be up front about the limits of your budget and insurance. If a therapist is not able to provide their own services directly, they will likely be able to point you in the right direction towards obtaining services that are covered by your insurance and/or are a good fit for your budget. Don't use cost as an excuse to give up hope of acquiring professional help for your child. As your child continues to grow, the negative tendencies may worsen. You're best off getting as much help as you can as soon as you can.

## *What to Expect In-Session*

When treating an ODD child, a therapist will strive to assess all contributing factors that may lead to the child's misbehavior. Emotions are often a big focus of therapy for ODD, as most ODD children struggle profoundly with emotional expression. They're prone to emotional outbursts, tantrums, screaming, or outward physical aggression. Standard anger management and relaxation techniques that will help the child learn how to calm himself are provided. Older children may be taught to identify triggers, things that set them off, and how to intercept this anger before it develops into a harmful expression. In therapy ODD children will also work on socialization by developing techniques to help them interact with, relate to, and be tolerant of both their peers and authority figures.

In terms of medication, while there is no specific pharmaceutical used for the treatment of ODD, ODD children may receive prescriptions for antidepressants or stimulants depending on what underlying emotional conditions are identified during the therapy process. In general medications aren't used for ODD children unless there's another disorder that's been clearly identified.

# Chapter 3: Understanding the Traits of a Strong Parent

Returning to our friend Rhonda and her plight to care for her ODD son, Jacob — remember this story is based on the true life story of a Southern California family dealing with ODD. Jacob ended up living at home with Rhonda and her husband, Clint, long after he was expelled from his high school. Rhonda and Clint talked about emancipating him at 17, but eventually decided that he was better off at home. He had no discernable skills or career aptitudes and they couldn't bear the thought that he might end up homeless and/or alcoholic. Thankfully, the drinking had subsided somewhat, but the anger did not. There was one occasion when Jacob became upset with his mom for insisting that he wash the truck — a vehicle that Jacob regularly used — that he began throwing things in the kitchen, including sharp knives. Clint was at work, and Rhonda was legitimately frightened, so much so that she ended up calling the police.

Having two officers show up at his residence was a definite wake-up call for Jacob, who was beginning to realize that his behavior had consequences and that his mother wasn't going to stand for it any longer. What really helped Jacob, however, was a random opportunity that was presented to him by a friend, who thought he might do well applying for work as truck loader at the nearby United Parcel Service hub. Though it wasn't easy getting Jacob to go through the interview process, he was enticed enough by the prospect of earning money that he followed through all the way to getting hired. Jacob had so much angry energy that he ended up loading trucks faster than anyone else on the dock, and the UPS job turned into a long time gig.

Over time, Jacob's mother noticed that his behavior had calmed. He still had a bit of a surly, snarky attitude, but his outbursts were contained and limited to raising his voice from time to time there was no more yelling, throwing of objects, choking, or kicking of the family dog.

As we can see from Jacob's case, pride, purpose, and self-esteem are truly the best treatment options for ODD over the long term. For Jacob, knowing that he was good at something, earning money from it and the respect of his parents and supervisors took away from his need to act out emotionally. But what if Jacob had been a horrible truck loader? Would it have been yet another blow to Jacob's already fragile self-esteem? An impetus for more anger, more outbursts, and more chaos? It's not always going to be readily apparent what will work and what won't work for an ODD child. You have to keep trying different things out.

Rhonda should be applauded for her actions. Involving the local authorities took a lot of courage. Rhonda surely feared that Jacob would never trust her again, but at the same time, he had crossed a line and was putting her in danger. It was also important for Jacob to know, as he veered closer to adulthood, that his actions would have consequences.

For parents dealing with an ODD child, strength, patience, and persistence are valuable assets. The behavior of ODD children will wear you down severely over time. If you are to conquer this disorder, then you have to be strong in your resolve. You have to be clear and consistent in your instructions to your children. As was previously mentioned, even if they don't want to admit it, children need their parents to provide them with a sense of stability and direction. If you fail to give that to them, it could easily result in the child's adversarial behavior worsening over time.

We know that having a child with ODD can be a challenge, especially when they're young, strong-willed and bursting with energy that you don't have. The strong parent is not the one who attempts to go tit for tat with their teenager in a shouting match, but the one who is able to calmly assess a situation and stick to her parenting principles. When you're consistent, strong and fair, your children will end up being less threatened by you. They will see less of the uncertainty in you that they feel and fear within themselves. They will turn to you for direction rather than trying to resist you.

Try to avoid thinking of your ODD child as simply stubborn or difficult. The broader truth is that they don't understand themselves and don't understand how to express their angst in a healthy way, so they resort to baiting their parents, teachers or other authority figures into power struggles, so that they might capture some feeling of control for having thwarted the demands of an authority figure, regardless of how prudent those demands might have been. When it's clear that your ODD child wants to engage you in a power struggle, you can show strength by realizing that it takes the participation of two parties to engage in a struggle against one another. If you refrain from engaging your child in anger and resist their efforts to entangle you in argument, then you will be able to subtly lead the way towards a more peaceful home, and your child, inevitably, will follow.

Parents show strength by communicating clearly with a consistent message. An ODD child requires continuous clarification of limits and rules. Your child must understand and remember everything you say, but you should also provide him with enough choices to give him a sense of freedom.

Show strength by knowing the difference between arguing and genuine discussion. The ODD child will often be verbally combative for its own sake. If your child questions your rules, judgments or requests in a thoughtful, respectful manner, then and only then should you take the time to explain yourself.

ODD children have a tendency to feel smothered by an authoritative presence, and when they feel that the threat is too much for them to bear, they resist. You show strength by controlling yourself in the face of this resistance. Even when you're doing everything right on your end, setting and communicating clear limits, controlling your anger and so on, things still don't always go as planned. The ODD child will still, at times, display aggression towards you. Stay strong, by staying in control and not resorting to anger.

Show strength by giving your child freedom to express himself and his opinions in a calm respectful manner. Set limits, sure, but don't try to dictate how your child thinks and feels. Being able to trust your child and give him freedom to be his own person and make his own decisions is a sign of strength, just as long as the behaviors he chooses don't fall afoul of the limits you've set. It's easy for parents to practice reactive parenting, simply disciplining their child when they do things wrong. Proactive parenting is about instilling positive values and direction and giving him a chance to earn freedom, respect and personal authority. Proactive parenting, when practiced, prevents problems before they happen and is a more meaningful show of strength than reactive parenting is. While it's good to set limits and discipline consistently, if that's all you're doing then your only attending to the symptoms of ODD, not the cause.

# Here are five common traits shown by strong parents:

## 1. Strong Parents Respect Their Children

Strong parents don't see their children as subservient beings who must heed their every demand. Children are human beings too with feelings, a voice, a unique worldview, opinions to offer, and characteristics to be appreciated.

## 2. Strong Parents Show Signs of Authority

Strong parents are able to maintain authority while also communicating to their child that they are earnestly looking out for his well-being. Being able to exhibit this kind of strength with an ODD child is an exceptional challenge, since the ODD child is not equipped to recognize the benign intentions of an authority figure. When caring for an ODD child, it's important to remember that just because your child is acting out and defiant, it doesn't mean you're a weak parent, as long as you're doing all you can to exhibit qualities of benign authority.

## 3. Strong Parents Know How to Show Affection

Being strong is showing compassion, acceptance and affection to your child. When a child feels that he is loved and accepted for who and what he is, he will be more inclined to respond positively to you. For parents of ODD children, showing affection can be a little more difficult. Be sure to seek out and act on opportunities to show affection to your ODD child. He needs as much assurance from you as he can get in order to internalize that you hold his best interests at heart.

## 4. Strong Parents Know How to Communicate With Their Children

Strong parents will know how to talk with their children, and how to keep the lines of communication open between them. One of the oversights a lot of parents make when dealing with an ODD child is over-engaging them in arguments rather than just listening. For ODD children, especially teenagers, they're, at-heart, less interested in getting their way and more interested in just being listened to. Sometimes they just want to vent and be heard. Learn how to distinguish when an answer or an argument is warranted and when your child is essentially just asking to be heard for a while.

## 5. Strong Parents Let Go of the Past

A strong parent will not allow the events of the past to determine how he or she will handle the child. Letting go of the past is hard, but in order to be strong, you will have to do so. With ODD children, you're going to undergo a long, hard road full of outbursts and at times downright abusive attacks. Take it one day at a time with the goal of having your child's behavior improve over the long run. What's great about children is that their attitudes, personalities and behavioral habits are still highly malleable. Be patient. Let go of the past. You'll get through it.

# Chapter 4:  How to Face Challenges

If you're parenting an ODD child, then you need to accept the fact that you're facing a more difficult challenge than is faced by most parents. This can be difficult for us to wrap our heads around, because all children have their unique challenges and most parents will agree that the act of parenting is the most, challenging endeavor they've ever undertaken. On the other extreme, you don't want your child's ODD condition to become an excuse for you to tolerate and excuse poor behavior.

As a parent you should strive to cultivate a *locus of control* that fully encompasses your own behavior and decisions. *Locus of control* is a term used in psychology, invented by Julian B. Rotter, used to describe the extent to which individuals believe themselves to be in control of the events that surround and affect them. A poor locus of control is present when an individual believes himself to be a victim of outside circumstances and that his or her own choices have little or no consequence. For the parent of an ODD child, it's at times tempting to throw in the towel and believe that no matter how hard you try to be a good parent your efforts will end up lost on your child. This is why it's important that you strive to localize your locus of control when it comes to dealing with your ODD child. Accept that your child has a disorder and is not going to be as responsive, even to good parenting. If you can still manage to be a good parent, then you're doing your part. You're controlling what you can control. If you try to extend your locus of control to include the behavior, attitudes and actions of your ODD child, then you're setting yourself up for failure and frustration.

An effective ODD parent doesn't tolerate or excuse poor behavior from their child, but neither do they blame themselves excessively for it. Sensitive people are sensitive parents. If you have a tendency to take things personally, then you'll likely find parenting an ODD child to be that much more challenging. Without obtaining professional support for yourself, you may end up becoming worn out or in a state of constant frustration. If this is the case, and you feel relentlessly infuriated, beaten up, or even depressed, then be sure to allow yourself plenty of breaks during which you can spend some time by yourself in order to recuperate and rejuvenate.

## Two-Parent Households and ODD

Much of this book may have seemed to speak to the problem of ODD from the perspective of the single parent. In general, the principles discussed in this book should apply to two - parent households. Even though a single parent can manage an ODD child effectively, a two-parent household, where the parenting partners function well together, is able to handle ODD children more effectively than single-parents.

One thing to avoid in a two-parent household with an ODD child is for both parents to confront the child head-on, so as to give the impression of ganging up or outnumbering the child. ODD children are already innately sensitive and errantly frightened of authoritative presence. If both parents are perceived to be attacking the child, then the child is likely to become even more fearful and tense, and his impulse to resist will manifest itself strongly, making it even harder to get through.

One of the great benefits of having a partner when caring for an ODD child is that you'll have someone to access for your own personal support. Sharing the struggle with a partner will help reduce the level of depression you feel due to challenging interactions with your child. Your shoulders will feel lighter, you'll walk with more bounce in your step, and it will be easier for you to stick to your parenting principles and to maximize your effectiveness in dealing with your child.

Avoid a good cop/bad cop routine when dealing with an ODD child. To make the biggest difference for your child, he needs to respect and trust both parents and not feel as if he can only safely communicate with one or the other.

ODD children can take you and your partner off guard. They're prone to say and do outrageous things, all while believing that they're completely justified in their behavior. He will shout at the top of his lungs. He will defy your orders. He will throw things. He will embarrass you in public. If at all possible, try to avoid meting out any punishment or substantive punishment until you've had a chance to discuss the situation and reflect with your partner.

While there's an undeniable advantage to having a good partner to assist you as you strive to care for your ODD child, it's entirely possible for a single parent to obtain good results as well. Single parents can look for support from friends or family members, as well as from professional therapists. At the end of the day, it's all about getting good support. Some people can find it in their marriage, for others it's their best friend, don't worry so much about having the perfect support model, just appreciate and take advantage of what's available to you, and seek professional help early on in your journey with ODD.

It is important to ensure that your emotions are being watched 24/7. If you feel that you are out-of-whack emotionally, have your partner take full control of interacting with your ODD child. In the first chapter of this book we discussed how your own personal history and the circumstances in which they grew up could profoundly affect your parenting methods and sensibilities. One tendency that parents have is to project themselves onto their children.

They see their children as their second chance, a way to remedy everything that went wrong in their lives. When parents who have this tendency are faced with the challenge of raising an ODD child, the results can be very problematic. Children have the capability to pick up on subtle disapproval, and given the ODD child's already vigilant temperament towards authority, any added negative pressures will only make your journey more difficult.

Focus on seeing your child as his own contained and sovereign person. Doing so will help you accept and not blame yourself for his ODD, while also preventing you from projecting your own identity onto your child.

## Putting the Past behind You

Today's a new day. Stop carrying around the guilt of yesterday. If you make a mistake when dealing with your ODD child, get used to it, forgive yourself, say you're sorry and move on. Many parents make the mistake of becoming hesitant to try and intervene in their ODD child's development after they become dissatisfied with or ashamed of their previous attempts and missteps. The ODD child may be inclined to exploit this insecurity by bringing up past events where you failed or miss-stepped as a parent. Do not let this happen. If you apologized and did everything within reason to make amends, then move on. Don't dwell on the past. Learn from your mistakes and allow the experience to help you become a better parent.

# Chapter 5: Five Key Skills to Adopt and Develop

Too many parents try to gain "cool points" with their children. As children get older, they will no longer want their parents to be their friends, but they will still need them to be their parents. The parenting job is hard. It's 24/7 and doesn't pay. But the rewards surpass anything this universe has to offer. The ODD child is one of the most challenging of all the parenting puzzles. Your ODD child will yell at you. He'll tell you he hates you. He'll test you and exploit your weak points to a point that would seem to challenge the patience of even the Dalai Lama, Mahatma Gandhi, or the Buddha himself. And it's somehow become your job to assume the incredibly difficult role of caring for this child.

When you stay confident and positive, and when you introduce the right tools and materials, the child will respond favorably. The child must also be made to feel accountable for his own actions. ODD children are not completely oblivious to everything that they do. Don't treat them as such and don't let them fool you by using ignorance as an excuse. Do you have to be the perfect parent? No, but you can be a good one. Here are five key attributes that will help you be the parent you need to be for your ODD child.

## 1. Set Limits

Remember that limitations should not be the sole basis for raising your ODD child. Opportunities must also be present. If the child feels that the rules have been set just to oppress him and control his life, then the child will want to rebel. Strive to give your child as much freedom and autonomy within those limits so that he might explore the world in the way he sees fit. Give him a chance to make up his opinions, make his own mistakes and learn his own lessons. Make sure your child knows the reason for these rules and limitations, that they've been established for his own good. Don't entertain arguments and tantrums, but do reward your child for thoughtful inquisitiveness.

## 2. Get to Know Your Child

Telling a parent that they need to take time to get to know their child may seem a bit unnecessary. After all, you've been with your child since he was a swaddling infant. You're going to know him from the inside out, better than anyone. Right? Not always. Children develop, learn and change at a fast pace, and when parents pay close attention, they will often discover new aspects of their children's inner universe that they've missed previously. ODD children can be exceptionally enigmatic, as they themselves are quite confounded by their own place in the world around them.

It's also healthy to keep in mind how different your child is when compared to his siblings. This should go without saying, but avoid comparing your children with one another, especially when one of your children is ODD. Never tell an ODD child that he needs to be more like his siblings, as it will severely erode his self-confidence. Sometimes it's helpful to forget for a moment that your child is yours and try getting to know him instead as you'd get to know someone whom you've just met. Ask him questions. Ask for his opinion on different issues. Show him that his personal autonomy is both recognized and respected.

## 3. Be Your Child's Role Model

Your child should want to be like you when he grows up. You should be a superhero to your child, and not just another adult. Even if your child is ODD and you're put in a position where you have to continuously confront and correct him, it's important that you do all you can to prevent your child from seeing you as his enemy. Ask yourself every night before going to bed if you did all you could do to be the best parent you could be.

## 4. Show Your Child You Love Him

This is probably the most important advice of all. If the child feels that you don't love him, then he will respond negatively towards you all the time. It's impossible to love your child too much. Show the child everyday that you love him by telling him so, or by playing with him, or participating in any activities he likes to take part in. This is not the same as spoiling, which is basically showering your child with material gifts, which is something you should not do. When the child feels loved, he responds positively.

## 5. Avoid Harsh Discipline

At all costs, parents should avoid disciplining their children using physical force and verbal intimidation as punishment. This type of disciplinary violence will only foster negative attitudes, even though it may correct a problem in the short term. In the long term, those negative attitudes will negatively alter the development of the child's personality. Ensure that all rules and limitations are explained to the fullest, so the child understands why he's being punished.

# Conclusion

Being a parent of a child with ODD is difficult and daunting. But the best way to handle these children and modify their behavior is by actually fixing yourself first. There's a way to thrive in the face of this problem and that's by recognizing that you're going to be much stronger for having encountered and dealt with it. If you're planning to have more children, then, no-doubt, having learned to care for an ODD child will make you a substantially stronger parent. Try to keep this in mind when you feel guilty for showering so much attention on your ODD child while perhaps your other children feel they're not getting adequate attention. This is going to be difficult for them as well. In the context of dealing with sibling jealousy, being able to point to a specified condition, such as "ODD" can be helpful for your other children as they strive to understand the behavior of their sibling and to not take it personally, all while understanding why you, at times, are going to be more patient, more forgiving, and less expectant towards the ODD child. Find ways to reward and recognize your other children. Enlist their support as you seek to care for your ODD child. Explain to them that they, like you, must access a higher realm of patience and compassion, so all of you, as a family, can make it through this difficult situation.

There is no magical drug to take for this disorder, in fact there is no formal pharmaceutical offering recognized specifically for the treatment of ODD. The onus falls back on the parents, teachers, therapist etc. to ensure that the ODD child receives the direction he needs. If parents wish to receive specific ODD training, then there are people such as psychologists, social workers, guidance counselors, spiritual advisors and psychiatrists, who are qualified to provide services for both the parents and the child.

But in order to treat the child, the child must first be understood. The fact that the child's personality is different from everyone else's must be taken into consideration. The parents must remain strong in their dealings with the child; so that they can stand firm, yet at the same time, provide a loving and supportive home environment.

Finally, I'd like to thank you for purchasing this book! If you found it helpful, I'd greatly appreciate it if you'd take a moment to leave a review on Amazon. Thank you!